T0199029

I Am Thankful
Yo Estoy Agradecido

Written by Karina Jacob

Illustrated by Victoria Bruno

Copyright © 2020 Karina Jacob.

All rights reserved. No part of this book may be used or reproduced by any means, graphic, electronic, or mechanical, including photocopying, recording, taping or by any information storage retrieval system without the written permission of the author except in the case of brief quotations embodied in critical articles and reviews.

This book is a work of non-fiction. Unless otherwise noted, the author and the publisher make no explicit guarantees as to the accuracy of the information contained in this book and in some cases, names of people and places have been altered to protect their privacy.

Balboa Press books may be ordered through booksellers or by contacting:

Balboa Press
A Division of Hay House
1663 Liberty Drive
Bloomington, IN 47403
www.balboapress.com
844-682-1282

Because of the dynamic nature of the Internet, any web addresses or links contained in this book may have changed since publication and may no longer be valid. The views expressed in this work are solely those of the author and do not necessarily reflect the views of the publisher, and the publisher hereby disclaims any responsibility for them.

Any people depicted in stock imagery provided by Getty Images are models, and such images are being used for illustrative purposes only.
Certain stock imagery © Getty Images.

Illustrated by Victoria Bruno

ISBN: 978-1-9822-5563-3 (sc)
ISBN: 978-1-9822-5564-0 (e)

Library of Congress Control Number: 2020918678

Print information available on the last page.

Balboa Press rev. date: 11/13/2020

BALBOA.PRESS
A DIVISION OF HAY HOUSE

I Am Thankful
Yo Estoy Agradecido

Through my journey of spiritual exploration, I felt inspired to write "I Am Thankful," a children's book about self-awareness. By sharing this experience with children, this book intends to light a little flame in their hearts and minds, to make a better world. It is a simple, fun, and uplifting bilingual book to enjoy with the whole family.

The following idea is in the content of the book:

Find things for which to be thankful in life and feel the love and joy expand in one's heart.

I am grateful for the loving support and encouragement of my family, friends, and teachers. I also want to thank Victoria for all her beautiful illustrations that make this book shine with love and talent.

A través de mi camino de exploración espiritual, me sentí inspirada a escribir "Yo Estoy Agradecido", un libro para niños sobre la conciencia de uno mismo. Al compartir esta experiencia con los niños, este libro intenta encender una pequeña llama en sus corazones y en sus mentes, para lograr un mundo mejor. Este es un libro bilingüe, simple, divertido y que eleva el espíritu, para disfrutarlo con la familia.

La siguiente idea está en el contenido del libro:

Encuentra cosas por las cuales estar agradecido en la vida y siente que el amor y la alegría se expanden en el corazón de uno.

Estoy agradecida por el amor, apoyo y aliento de mi familia, amigos y maestros. También agradezco a Victoria por sus hermosas ilustraciones que hacen que este libro brille con amor y talento.

I am thankful each day for the blessings I receive in my life.

Estoy agradecido cada día por las bendiciones que recibo en mi vida.

I am thankful for my family.

Estoy agradecido por mi familia.

I am thankful for my grandma and my grandpa.

Estoy agradecido por mi abuela y mi abuelo.

I am thankful for my aunt, my uncle, and my cousins.

Estoy agradecido por mi tía, mi tío y mis primos.

I am thankful for...
my home, my food, my room, my bed, my clothes, and my toys.

Estoy agradecido por ....
mi hogar, mi comida, mi habitación, mi cama, mis ropas y mis juguetes.

I am thankful for...
my school, my teachers, and my friends.

Estoy agradecido por...
mi escuela, mis maestros y mis amigos.

I am thankful for...
nature: the animals, the trees, the mountains, and the oceans.

Estoy agradecido por...

la naturaleza: los animales, los árboles, las montañas y los océanos.

I am thankful for the day and the night.

Estoy agradecido por el día y la noche.

I am thankful for the sun, the moon, and the stars.

Estoy agradecido por el sol, la luna y las estrellas.

I am thankful for the spring and the summer.

Estoy agradecido por la primavera y el verano.

I am thankful for the fall and the winter.

Estoy agradecido por el otoño y el invierno.

Every time I find things for which to be thankful, I feel the love and joy in my heart grow more and more!

¡Cada vez que encuentro algo para estar agradecido, siento que el amor y la alegría en mi corazón crecen más y más!

Karina Jacob, Author
Karina was born and raised in Asunción, Paraguay, which inspired her to write in English and Spanish. She is an early childhood educator and believes in the love that each one of us have in our hearts, and when we share it with others, we make the world a better place.

Karina nació y creció en Asunción, Paraguay, lo cual le inspiró a escribir en inglés y español. Ella es maestra de párvulos y cree en el amor que cada uno de nosotros tiene en el corazón, y cuando lo compartimos con los demás, hacemos que el mundo sea mejor.

Victoria Bruno, Illustrator
Victoria was born and raised in Santiago, Chile. A self-taught artist, she is an early childhood educator that loves to teach and create. She believes in freedom and mutual love. She dreams of a world full of colors where everyone can see their reflection in each other.

Victoria nació y creció en Santiago, Chile. Es una artista autodidacta y maestra de párvulos, que adora enseñar y crear. Ella cree en la libertad y el amor mutuo. Sueña con un mundo lleno de colores donde todos puedan verse reflejados en el otro.

Author's note

The character in this book is a child who, in a playful and fun way, represents each one of us readers and our potential to make a better world.

These times have made us grateful for things which we might have taken for granted, such as social and family gatherings, freedom of movement, live entertainment, human contact, etc.

When we are grateful and appreciative for what we have, for what is working out, and for all the beauty that surrounds us; the love and joy expand in our hearts, which uplift our being. These feelings produce the natural feel-good chemicals in our bodies that enhance our well-being. In this state, we can become empowered and shift our life experience, as we can now be open to the vast goodness that life has to offer.

El personaje de este libro es un niño que, de una manera juguetona y divertida, representa a cada uno de nosotros, los lectores y nuestro potencial para hacer un mundo mejor.

Esta época nos ha vuelto agradecidos por cosas que podríamos haber dado por hecho, tales como reuniones sociales y familiares, libertad de movimiento, entretenimiento en vivo, contacto humano, etc.

Cuando agradecemos y apreciamos lo que tenemos, lo que está yendo bien y toda la belleza que nos rodea; el amor y la alegría se expanden en nuestros corazones, los cuales elevan nuestro ser. Estos sentimientos generan los químicos naturales que nos hacen sentir bien, realzando nuestro bienestar. En este estado, podemos fortalecernos y cambiar nuestra experiencia de vida, ya que ahora podemos estar abiertos a todo lo bueno que la vida tiene para ofrecer.

Printed in the United States
By Bookmasters